# Outsource Your Marketing

## Want my help implementing the content in this book?

My goal is to save you hundreds of hours and thousands of dollars in the marketing process— and to help you create more freedom in your life so you can focus on what you actually love doing.

Leave the marketing to the experts.

If you want to go further and move faster, and you're serious about getting our help, book a call with our team to create a plan and see how we can help.

www.jendevore.rocks/apply

# Outsource Your Marketing

*Reach More Prospects,*
*Scale Faster, and Work Less*

JEN DEVORE RICHTER, M.A.

Paperback ISBN-13: 978-1-7329956-1-1
eBook ISBN-13: 978-1-7329956-2-8

## To My Husband, Will

*Thank you for being my biggest supporter throughout the ups and downs of entrepreneurship. You've been there for both the standing ovations and the moments when I've cried on your shoulder. I'm grateful for everything you do for our family and for me.*

## To My Clients

*This book was 100% inspired by the brave entrepreneurs I have the honor of calling my clients. Every day, you wake up committed to making a difference despite the hassles from the suits in ivory towers telling us it can't be done. I believe the world is changed by entrepreneurs, and it will continue to evolve due to your messages and influence. If given the opportunity to speak your mind freely, the status quo will change. It is my honor to work alongside you as you share your ideas and reach people with your important work.*

# Table of Contents

# Before You Begin

The purpose behind this book is simple: It is to share insider knowledge that you need to build effective Outsourced Marketing Systems (OMS) that lead to both great results in your business and also give you the time and freedom you so desperately seek as an entrepreneur.

The reason I know you desperately seek time and freedom is because I know what it's like to own a business! If you weren't motivated by freedom, you would get a corporate job and work for someone else, but here you are. You're trying to run a business and tackle all of the tasks and daily activities related to business ownership. The thing you love the most about being an entrepreneur is working with your clients. You love seeing their faces light up when your solutions work for them. You love hearing the positive feedback they share after working with you and seeing their lives change.

I can also predict that the thing you hate the most about being a business owner is marketing. I get it. If you didn't go to school for marketing or you haven't studied it for your entire adult life, it can be so frustrating. Marketing feels like a moving target that is impossible to catch. There are tech headaches, constantly changing algorithms, and expensive tools to buy, and it's hard to know whom to trust when hiring people to help you.

Because of all of this mystery in marketing, most entrepreneurs end up relying on word-of-mouth to grow their businesses. They will wake up every week, for years, at 5 a.m. to attend networking meetings instead of doing the professional development work it takes to master marketing. Although attending networking meetings may be fruitful for some, for most of us it is a dead-end road because it is not a scalable activity. You, as a business owner, are a hot commodity in your profession, and your time needs to be spent on business growth, creating systems, and finding people to run your systems for you. That is the way to build a business you love while also giving you true freedom in your life.

Alternatively, perhaps you have invested tens of thousands of dollars in a bloated marketing agency, hoping that if you just threw enough money at the problem it would solve itself. But investing more money into your marketing by relinquishing it to an agency isn't necessarily the right answer either.

Most entrepreneurs think they're doing enough marketing by simply going to networking events and trying to land clients one at a time. Just like throwing money at an ad agency, and making them deal with the marketing (instead of leading and creating a system for a team to manage), this is usually unsuccessful.

What you're experiencing and feeling is common, but it does not need to be permanent. You do not need to let analysis paralysis or fear of failure hold you back from creating an Outsourced Marketing System (OMS) that works.

In this book, I will share six perspective shifts that are vital in helping you make better marketing decisions. These perspective shifts come from my work as an entrepreneur and an award-winning marketing coach who has worked with hundreds of business owners from various backgrounds. My clients are doctors, lawyers, advisors, agents, coaches, speakers, publishers, and others. While their businesses appear to be different, in actuality their problems are more similar than you'd think. When it comes to marketing, nearly all businesses have the same problems. These six perspective shifts come from speaking with, working with, and helping entrepreneurs from all over the world who are just like you. I have seen the radical transformations that take place once these paradigm shifts happen and their minds are renewed.

As a fellow entrepreneur, I know your time is valuable and you feel like you are constantly running out of time. My goal with this book is to cut the fluff and tell you *exactly* what you need to know and nothing more. Your goal should be to read this book and gain an understanding of marketing like you've never had before so that you can make better decisions when it comes to knowing exactly what systems need to be put in place, who to hire, how much money should be spent, and which tools you need—and which ones you don't.

My promise is that, after reading this book, you should be able to implement these proven ideas within twenty-four hours to start seeing immediate results in time-savings, cost-savings, or outcomes.

If there is a question you would like answered, please reach out to me personally at jen@jendevore.com or join our free Facebook group at https://www.facebook.com/groups /instantmediamogul

To your success!
*Jen DeVore Richter*

# CHAPTER 1

# Mindset Matters

*Limiting Belief:*
I'm a service provider, not a marketer.

**TRUTH:**
You are a marketer of services, not just
a provider.

Having the right attitude and mindset toward marketing and selling will make or break you as an entrepreneur. It's not enough to see yourself solely as a provider of the service you offer; you also must see yourself as a *marketer* of the service you offer. This is an important distinction and an integral key to your success and survival as an entrepreneur.

- You are not a chiropractor. You are a *marketer* of chiropractic services.
- You are not a real estate agent. You are a *marketer* of home buying/selling services.

- You are not a doctor. You are a *marketer* of health services.
- You are not a coach. You are a *marketer* of coaching services.
- You are not a home contractor. You are a *marketer* of home contracting services.
- You are not a _____. You are a marketer of _____ services.

This perspective shift might be difficult to grasp because, unfortunately, they don't teach marketing in most chiropractic colleges, law schools, real estate certification classes, coaching certification programs, or most other professional-service programs. Here's the harsh reality: the people who sit in the ivory towers and create course curricula are usually academics who have no idea what it takes to make it in the real world.

When people graduate from these programs, they are well trained to do the activities needed for daily work; however, they weren't taught how to land clients. What I see most often is professionals who are highly educated in their specific areas of expertise. But when they hang their shingles, they face the very real possibility of having to go work for someone else because they were never taught marketing at a highly effective level.

Some industries pass down standards of practice like tales around a campfire. These often include advice regarding getting business cards printed up, creating a website, joining a networking group, and asking everyone you know if they want to do business with you. This results in a negative attitude and mindset towards marketing because, although there is a lot of activity involved, the results are not often fruitful.

The education system is failing at teaching people who want to own a business how to make money, which is why you should invest in self-study books like this one.

## "That's Not How It's Done in My Industry."

The standards of practice that are passed around like hot potatoes, from one person to another, result in a fixed mindset. This mindset is often expressed in the phrase, "That's not how it's done in my industry." It is one of the most dangerous perspectives about marketing that a business owner can possess.

Even if most of the people in your industry suffer from failing businesses and are saddled with debt, there will still be a mindset that does not embrace new ideas or being different. This limiting belief keeps businesses from succeeding, and industries from progressing, because the secret to success is to do the *exact opposite* of what everyone else in your industry is doing. Yes, you read that correctly: the secret to marketing success is to do what others in your industry are *not* doing.

If your competition has not embraced video marketing, make videos. Start publishing books and magazines, if this isn't already being done. Even if sending emails has a bad reputation in your industry, do it anyway. The only way to stand out and get attention in a crowded market is to dare to be different.

Dr. Lynn Tran and Dr. Sam McDonald are a married chiropractic duo based in Denver, Colorado, who successfully overcame the mindset of just being providers of healthcare services by becoming *marketers* of healthcare services.

When I first met with them, they expressed their love of patient care and frustration with not having a predictable way of building awareness and generating new business. Dr. McDonald was relying on early-morning networking groups as a way of getting the word out. This tactic was working marginally, at best. Meanwhile, Dr. Tran had become entrenched in organizing a community event for which she was not getting the credit she deserved.

The first marketing challenge we tackled was how to help them become Denver's "brain health experts" by creating more valuable and helpful content on the internet than what was being offered by their local competition. They both committed to scaling their marketing efforts by posting video content, primarily on their YouTube channel, to build awareness of the symptoms and problems commonly faced by their prospective patients. For months, they have consistently created and posted content, including long-form and short-form videos, and sent a weekly email to their list. They are enjoying YouTube success in search engine results, and now hold high rankings for their important key terms. They've also had an increase in new patients and hear frequently that their videos have increased awareness of their services.

By seeing themselves in their new identity—not just as providers of chiropractic care but as experts who have important knowledge to share with their community—they have created a scalable and predictable Marketing System that will grow as they do. I am so proud of them for being open to sharing their expertise with their wider community. They are impacting lives daily by creating videos that help people with their most pressing health concerns and getting the word out about their business in a scalable way.

## Combatting Imposter Syndrome: Putting Yourself Out There

My dad was in the US Air Force for over 25 years, so I grew up with constant new-kid syndrome. (It's not really a syndrome; I just made it up to prove a point.)

Most people don't know this about me, but I was born in England and didn't move to the states full-time until I was about nine years old. Both of my little brothers were born overseas too. One brother was born in England, like me, and the other was born in Germany.

On the one hand, growing up as an "Air Force brat" and moving every couple of years was exciting. We had a new adventure before us all the time! On the other hand, it was a total drag.

Here's what is a drag about being the new kid in school:

- You never know if your school clothes are "cool" for the region you live in.

- You don't know who to hang out with and who is bad news.
- You feel ostracized and alone on that first day when you walk into school because everyone knows each other.
- At first, it's awkward finding kids to eat lunch with.

Here's what is cool about being the new kid in school:

- If you were unpopular at the old school, you have a chance to change that.
- You get to experience places and people very few others (including grown adults) get to experience in their entire lives.
- You become adept at change and nothing throws you off.
- You get to reset the terms for who you are, who your friends are, and what you're about.

I used to think that being the new kid all the time was super annoying. But now, as an adult and a business owner, I'm glad that I had that experience because it has helped me overcome moments of self-doubt and imposter syndrome.

Like being the new kid in school, being the new expert on the scene in your industry can often result in similar thoughts: What will people say or think when I show up like *that*? If I do show up and step up, will people take me seriously?

What I found from being the perpetual new kid is that people will respect you if you show up authentically—as your true self.

When I tried to fit in with the cool kids and wear clothes that weren't my style, it showed on my face. I looked and felt uncomfortable, and like a fraud.

When I wore what I wanted and showed up authentically, I gained acceptance.

The same is true for a business owner.

When I try to fit into someone else's mold, I feel uncomfortable, and it shows.

When I show up as myself (the good, the bad, and the ugly), I feel comfortable, and it shows.

## Show Up Authentically to Avoid Imposter Syndrome

One of the success hacks I share with my clients is to notice others who are successful and try to learn from them. If your business is struggling, it's easier and faster to invest in coaching or training with someone who has been there, done that, and been victorious, instead of trying to figure it out on your own.

But coaching and training are just the foundation on which you need to build; it's critical to know what is different about you, and infuse your own style and substance into your business.

Every time I decide to change my business model or integrate a new marketing strategy, I take my own advice and hire the best in the business. I was trained by the world's best speak-to-sell trainers at Speaking Empire. I joined the legendary "Godfather of Direct Response Marketing" Dan Kennedy's organization Magnetic Marketing and was one of a handful of Certified Magnetic Marketing Advisors for a few years. I was even trained by an Emmy award–winning TV producer on how to be a great TV show host and guest because I knew it would help me on podcasts, radio shows, and TV segments.

When I lost my career as a keynote speaker in 2020 (due to lockdowns) and decided to go all-in on YouTube, I invested in the best YouTube coaches. I invested in myself, absorbed all the information, and practiced and trained using their proven techniques. Once I had the basics down, I added my own approach to everything that I had learned.

Now I get lots of phone calls from other business coaches and consultants who want to know my secret to success. They call and ask me to send them my pricing sheet, they sign up for my webinars to hack my flow, and they subscribe to my email list and Facebook group to see what I send to my community.

But here's what's wrong with that approach: how I run my business is different from how they should run their businesses because they have a uniqueness that is inherent to only them—and so do I.

Also, there is more to it than what is seen on the surface. There are reasons why my prices are set where they are; there are reasons why I have each slide in my webinar; there are reasons why I share certain personal stories with my email list.

It's true that to become known as the go-to expert in your business, you will need to consult with and be trained by the best! But you will also need to reveal what makes you unique and add that to a solid foundation of training and advice.

Showing up as your authentic self—and not just copying/pasting what your competition does—is key to avoid feeling like an imposter.

## Investing in Marketing vs. Spending Money on Marketing

Once you find your confidence and unashamedly start to see yourself as a *marketer* of your professional services, you will quickly realize that getting the marketing done at a high level of quality requires a real investment. You will need to invest in coaches, graphic designers, and editors; you will need to invest in new equipment, software programs, printing, and more. It's important for you to know this significant but simple fact: whoever spends the most money on marketing wins.

However, spending money on marketing doesn't mean just throwing money at ads, building a new website, or hiring an SEO guru. Investing in marketing goes much deeper than that. The primary goal as a marketer is not to figure out how to do things by spending the least but to figure out how to do things even if it means you spend the most.

Now, this doesn't mean you throw money at marketing, hoping for something to stick. Instead, you must create an irresistible offer (what you sell that people want), have a Market Dominating Position, or MDP, (a clear differentiation), and be confident in the problem you solve and for whom you solve it. Once this is done, it is wise to invest as much of your time and resources as possible in your marketing. Also, instead of just attending your professional association conferences, you will want to keep up with the latest strategies and know what's working now (and what isn't) by attending the best marketing conferences in the world.

I love this story of an entrepreneur friend of mine. Roger Wakefield is a Texas-based plumber who wanted to learn how to use social media to grow his business, so he registered for a video conference. Upon checking in, one of the event organizers remarked that Roger was the only trade professional registered to attend. At that moment, Roger knew he was on to something. He was right. What he learned at that video marketing conference forever changed his life. Fast forward a few years, and Roger now has over *five hundred thousand* subscribers on his YouTube channel and has amassed quite a large social media following. He is frequently asked to speak and present his ideas at conferences for entrepreneurs and marketers. Roger started to see himself as a marketer of plumbing expertise instead of only a plumber. Because of that mindset shift, he is helping families worldwide learn how to solve their plumbing problems with his videos that teach homeowners how to solve their simple plumbing issues without having to hire a plumber. By changing his mindset about marketing, Roger changed his life.

## Understanding the Lifetime Value of a Client

As a marketer, another key concept for you to fully understand related to spending money on marketing is the lifetime value of a client.

Let me explain.

If you have to spend $500 to land a client, but that one client is worth $20,000 to $100,000, or more, over their

## *DO THIS NOW!*

Take a few minutes to calculate the average lifetime value of your best client using the space below:

$ _____ Average Transaction Sale Price

x _____ Number of Transactions Per Year

x _____ Number of Years You Retain Them

= $ _____ Your Average Lifetime Value of a Client

### *Ask yourself this question:*
How much are you willing to spend to land a client at that value?

$_____

lifetime, it would be the best $500 you would ever spend. Most people with a limited mindset towards marketing look at the $500 as an expense, not an investment. This is a major mistake and a negative mindset to be avoided. Also, many business owners don't have a systematic way of keeping clients long enough beyond an initial transaction.

I see this in the coaching industry and professional services, where hourly rates are common. For example, hourly experts will advertise that their coaching or consulting service is $100 per hour. Their marketing and sales systems will be set up where they mostly focus on transactional business, and they are happy if they land a client who books one or two sessions.

A better way to approach this business model is to create a program that has recurring payments built into it. For example, sell a package with a minimum of four sessions in it or sell a year-long program that has recurring payments that are made every month. With the same amount of effort put toward your marketing, you could take your $200 client and turn them into a $12,000 (or more) client. With a few tweaks to your approach, you could increase the lifetime value of your client by fifty times or more. If you provide amazing value and results for your clients, you should be able to hang on to them for years, resulting in a much larger lifetime value.

Implementing this approach in a service-based business does require an important change in your mindset. You must see yourself as a marketer of your services and not just a provider of services.

# *Success Story*

Karen Johnson is the only female custom home builder in Houston, Texas. Her industry is male dominated and thick with old-school patterns and ways of doing business that do not tend to be very "touchy feely" or detail oriented. Karen wanted to break out of the mold and leverage her difference as a female business owner. We worked with Karen to publish her own home design magazine that she offers for free on her website and in hard-copy format for sales consultations. This magazine is full of "before" and "after" photos of her projects, design ideas, and helpful tips for homeowners to use when hiring a home contractor. Within two weeks of publishing this free magazine, Karen landed a $40,000 kitchen remodeling job, and she continues to enjoy distinction for doing the opposite of what her competition is doing.

## Sales Has a Bad Reputation and How to Overcome It

I recently walked into a furniture store, looking to buy a new dresser. Immediately upon my arrival, the salesperson jumped in front of me with her clipboard in hand and started spewing out the store specials. I said, "No thank you," and started walking around the store. She proceeded to follow me around, lurking behind couches and floor plants like a cheetah hunting its prey. I left without buying a thing.

I checked my email this morning and had yet another unsolicited email, pitching services I have no interest in buying. Delete!

I checked my LinkedIn account and my inbox held *six* new pitches from strangers. I immediately blocked them all.

These common experiences give professional marketers and experienced sales professionals a bad reputation, but please don't let these bad apples ruin your perception of the power of effective sales and marketing.

The reason why these experiences leave a bad impression is that the people doing the pitching are missing one key component to marketing success: **you must match your marketing to the way people buy.**

# CHAPTER 2

# Strategy Outperforms Tactics Every Time

*Limiting Belief:*
That's not how it's done in my industry.

***TRUTH:***
Do the exact opposite strategy of your
competition and win.

n April 2019, my husband, Will, and I sold our home in
Florida, packed all of our belongings, and moved across
the country to Colorado. As new empty nesters, the personal and professional possibilities were wide open for us. My
husband quit his job, and I left a business that I had started
with two business partners. When we moved to Colorado, I
did not know a soul, professionally speaking. I had no net-
work, I had no reputation, and I had no strategy or systems in
place that would help me relaunch my career. That was when
I decided to become a professional keynote speaker and to

focus on making that role my main strategy to help me land consulting and coaching clients.

With the goal of being a keynote speaker and getting paid to speak at other people's events to build my audience and connections faster, one of the first actions I took once we were settled into our new home in Denver was to join the Colorado chapter of the National Speakers Association. I hoped that involvement in this organization would help me jump-start my success as a professional speaker. At my first chapter meeting, I met an individual who connected me with a local chamber of commerce who booked me as a keynote speaker for a women's leadership meeting. At that leadership meeting, I landed a client who became one of my most loyal and long-term clients. I also made connections and built relationships that still serve me today.

In March 2020, the coronavirus sidetracked my plans and completely wrecked my strategy of becoming a professional keynote speaker because live events were canceled, and we all were put on lockdown in our homes. So, although I'd had quick success with my new strategy of landing speaking engagements and booking high-value clients, I was forced to change my approach overnight.

At that time, I knew nothing about how to be successful on YouTube. I didn't know any of the tips and tricks, I didn't know which software programs I needed, I didn't know anything about tech setup, and I most definitely did not know how to build a team that could help me launch my YouTube career. What I did know was that transitioning to YouTube made sense because of my experience and skill set. I committed to making a YouTube strategy work for me.

Fast forward three years, and I now have YouTube's number one channel on "magazine publishing," according to VidIQ and YouTube search. Magazine publishing is a service that I offer through Instant Media Mogul, which is one of the businesses I own and operate. Having complete search domination for a major key term in my business has been life changing. I do not have to chase clients; instead, I pull them to me like a magnet. Strangers are searching on the internet for solutions to problems they have. Using my YouTube strategy, I have created a system that converts people from simply using YouTube as a resource to subscribing to my channel which, subsequently, leads them to hiring me as a speaker for their events. A scalable business was built in less than one year because of the right strategy.

Ultimately, my goal with the Instant Media Mogul magazine publishing business is to sell it in ten years or so. I am always considering the future in my marketing strategy. I look at my YouTube channel as a valuable asset and myself as the spokesperson of the channel. I am not so emotionally tied to the YouTube marketing strategy that I would ever let my ego get in the way of me selling it to another publishing company.

In the meantime, I am attracting wonderful clients who already know, like, and trust me because they've been binge watching my content. When I do Zoom consultations with my YouTube subscribers, they frequently mention how appreciative they are of my videos. They tell me that my video content is changing the game for them, and they are so grateful. They also will remark on how no one else is creating video content for magazine publishing. This is my favorite comment of all because it tells me that by doing the exact opposite of what my competition is doing, I'm doing something right.

The magazine publishing industry has a reputation for being outdated and not embracing the internet as quickly as other industries have. I used this perception of the industry to my advantage by coining the phrase "magazine funnel." A magazine funnel is a traditional printed magazine that is turned into a digital magazine with flipping pages that are delivered by a modern sales funnel. A magazine funnel helps entrepreneurs position themselves as authority figures in their businesses and gives them control over their own marketing, which means they are not reliant on platforms they do not own. A magazine funnel also helps traditional magazine publishers scale and grow their reach with contributors, resulting in more advertising revenue. By doing the opposite of my competition, I have claimed the number one spot in search engine results on YouTube for "magazine publishing." In 2019, I was named "Innovator of the Year" at an international conference for business coaches because of my unique approach. I beat out over 550 other coaches because

I dared to do what others had not. I was also interviewed on the *ClickFunnels* radio show and landed a coveted spot, discussing magazine funnels, on Dan Kennedy's Magnetic Marketing stage.

As a business owner, I have used my magazine funnel to build my email list faster, create recurring revenue through selling magazine ads, strengthen my relationships with joint venture partners, book myself as a speaker at national conferences for entrepreneurs, be interviewed on TV and radio programs, and more.

By doing the exact opposite of what my competition is doing, I have been able to grow faster, attract clients I adore, and build my industry authority as an expert. You can do this too. It just takes the right strategy and approach.

Previously, I mentioned the importance of having a Market Dominating Position (MDP). Let's talk about what an MDP is and why you need one. I will show you real-life examples and give you space to create your own.

## Strategy for Cultivating a Market Dominating Position (MDP)

What specific niche market or marketplace segment should your business focus on? Determining this involves combining the skills your business has with the unmet needs of your targeted prospects, and then designing your product or service to fulfill those needs.

# *DO THIS NOW!*

### *Step Number One:*
### *Determine Your Market Dominating Position*

WRITE YOURS HERE:

_____

### *Step Number Two:*
### *Determine Your Primary Market Dominating Position*

This is the most dominating advantage that separates you from your competitors. Examples:

- Domino's claimed it could deliver its pizza in thirty minutes or less, or they would give it to you for *free!*
- Instant Media Mogul turns a self-published magazine into more than fifty revenue-generating ideas for entrepreneurs.

### *Step Number Three:*
### *Determine Your Supporting Business Model. Examples:*

- To make good on their promise every time, Domino's Pizza was forced to create a supporting business model where they built low-cost, plain-vanilla stores that were strategically located near college campuses.

- To make good on our promise every time, Instant Media Mogul provides access to a proprietary marketing center with a list of ideas and copyright templates for clients to use and implement.
- To make good on this promise every time, [our company] will . . .

WRITE YOURS HERE:

_____

Please notice the important distinction between an Market Dominating Position and a tagline. A tagline is usually a meaningless phrase like "family owned for fifty years" or "best customer service." Big brands will say something like "just do it" or "have a Coke and a smile."

A tagline is *not* an Market Dominating Position Strategy. As a business owner, you don't *need* a tagline. You *need* an Market Dominating Position Market Dominating Position.

If you are stuck trying to develop your Market Dominating Position, it may be because you are thinking too broadly. A common trap that most entrepreneurs fall into is trying to work with "anyone who [fill in the blank.]" Powerful Market Dominating Position Strategies come from being clear and concise about what problem you solve and for whom.

Here's an example everyone knows: Domino's Pizza, offering fresh, hot pizza delivered to your door in thirty minutes or less, or it's free. Guaranteed.

Here are some MDP examples from the stories I shared previously:

Example #1: Denver's Brain Health Experts

Example #2: YouTube's number one channel on "magazine publishing"

Example #3: Houston's only female-owned and operated custom home builder

Example #4: The Expert Plumber

## Know What Keeps Your Customers Up at Night

If you do not know what problem you solve for your ideal, perfect customer, you need to understand the pain that keeps them up at night. One way to find this out is to conduct interviews with at least ten people who could be your ideal, perfect customers and simply ask them, "What is the problem that keeps you up at night?"

I was watching the local news one morning and saw a TV commercial for a powerful, local investment agent. The company's owner was standing in front of a plain blue background. He was dressed up in his finest suit, and you could tell that he was being directed. He was standing with his hands clenched in front of him and came across as just a regular guy, not a paid actor. What got my attention about this unassuming approach to advertising were the first words out of his mouth: "Is the fear of cash flow and unpaid taxes keeping you up at night?" As soon as he said these words, I knew he was speaking to business owners.

He described how business owners feel when they are worried about money. He nailed the commercial by tapping into the very real and common emotions faced by entrepreneurs from all walks of life and in nearly every industry. He did not talk about how many years he had been in business or what certifications he holds. He did not make the commercial about himself or his ego. As he wrapped up the commercial, he was very specific about asking for his ideal, perfect customer by saying, "If you are spending more than $100,000 in taxes every year, reach out for a free consultation." Then, he gave a clear call to action with his website and phone number.

As the TV commercial ended, the marketer in me was thinking about how powerful and effective this simple strategy must be. I can recognize great marketing when I see it, even if it doesn't come wrapped in a million-dollar production budget and a catchy tagline from a New York City advertising agency. A good messaging strategy will outperform fancy production tactics every time.

## Sell Cures, Not Preventions

Effective marketing sells cures, not preventions. People buy solutions to problems. Usually, these problems are in one of three broad areas: health, wealth, or relationships. To be effective with your marketing strategy, you need to point out how your service solves a pressing and big problem in one or more of those three categories. The bigger the problem you solve, the better.

The local investor mentioned above successfully related to the concerns entrepreneurs face regarding wealth and money. He specifically mentioned cash flow and taxes. Cash flow disruptions in a small business can result in the inability to make payroll or pay bills on time. Overpaying on taxes can result in less profit to reinvest back into the business for much-needed equipment. These are both huge problems that need to be addressed. On a secondary level, when business owners can't make payroll, this causes employees to leave to find work somewhere else. It could result in the business owner being so stressed out at night that they take it out on their spouse and end up in a failed marriage. Relationships can be impacted by money problems too. But, our investor didn't lead with the secondary issues because those are not problems his company directly solves.

## Value-Based Pricing Strategy

Before I implemented Value-Based Pricing in my business, I would spend hours responding to requests for proposals (RFPs) only to end up feeling taken advantage of when I didn't get the job. There was one instance when a potential client asked my agency to do a complete audit of his marketing

**DO THIS NOW!**

Which primary category does your business solve? (Health, wealth, or relationships)

WRITE YOURS HERE:

_____

Which secondary category does your business solve? (Health, wealth, or relationships)

WRITE YOURS HERE:

_____

strategy, and then present a proposal for how we would fix it and how much it would cost. Because we needed the business, I jumped at the opportunity and spent about a dozen hours auditing his website and digital presence, coming up with solutions, and creating custom pricing to fix it. Spoiler alert: I still didn't win the business! I found out later that he decided to hire an internal staff person, and she implemented many of our ideas. I swore then and there that I would again never chase clients by responding to an RFP. I have held true to my conviction without any sleepless nights. I now have clients I love who respect my time and ideas and pay me what I'm worth—without arguing.

Outsourcing your marketing becomes a lot easier when you know exactly what you sell, at what price, and to whom, and avoid creating custom solutions for every potential client who knocks on your door requesting a proposal. When you're creating systems and building a team, it's more productive and profitable for each step in the process to be focused on selling specific services.

Having a Value-Based Pricing strategy is a great way to simplify sales instead of responding to RFPs. I like the simple "good-better-best" approach for this strategy.

There is a phenomenon in sales where most people will pick the middle option if given three choices. So, let's begin there. To start, your middle offer is the "better" offer; it is your baseline transaction.

Let's use a three-tiered offer as an example to see how this could hypothetically look:

| GOOD | BETTER | BEST |
|---|---|---|
|  | *1-hour weekly consulting calls* |  |
|  | *Session recordings and action items offered* |  |
|  | *Access to online course* |  |
|  | *Access to digital vault of copyright-free templates* |  |

Notice that our core offer is not just an hourly rate for consulting. It is a bundled package with multiple items included to create more value for the client.

Now, while most people will pick the middle option if presented with three choices, there is also a percentage who will always choose the top option. These are the people who will pay more for special treatment, VIP experiences, and behind-the-scenes access.

Here's the table with the "best" option included:

| GOOD | BETTER | BEST |
|------|--------|------|
|  | *1-hour weekly consulting calls* | *1-hour weekly consulting calls* |
|  | *Session recordings and action items* | *Session recordings and action items* |
|  | *Access to online course* | *Access to online course* |
|  | *Access to digital vault of copyright-free templates* | *Access to digital vault of copyright-free templates* |
|  |  | *Unlimited email and text support* |
|  |  | *Access to 24/7/365 emergency helpdesk* |

We love our clients who choose "better" or "best" options, but, let's face it, not every prospect can afford our top packages. Let's create a "downsell" option for those folks. This is your "good" option.

Here's how that could look:

| GOOD | BETTER | BEST |
| --- | --- | --- |
| 1-hour weekly consulting calls | 1-hour weekly consulting calls | 1-hour weekly consulting calls |
| Session recordings and action items | Session recordings and action items | Session recordings and action items |
| | Access to online course | Access to online course |
| | Access to digital vault of copyright-free templates | Access to digital vault of copyright-free templates |
| | | Unlimited email and text support |
| | | Access to 24/7/365 emergency helpdesk |

Now that we have three set packages, we can shorten our sales process, make it clear to our customers and team what we sell and don't sell, and provide more value to customers.

## Real-Life Case Study

To further demonstrate why Value-Based Pricing is important, here is an example from my professional experience: Ana is an advanced registered nurse practitioner (ARNP) and medical director of a direct primary care business in Florida.

Direct primary care cuts out the headache of dealing with insurance companies and complicated billing, and provides fast, affordable, and effective primary care (and, in Ana's case, women's health services) using a cash-pay monthly membership model.

Ana has been an ARNP for over twenty years and is well known and loved in her community, so her trust factor is extremely high. But, when creating her new business model, Ana needed to clearly demonstrate the value of the membership plan in a way that was easy for potential patients to understand.

When Ana contacted me, her prices were listed on her website as $75 per month, but she lacked a clear description of the *value* her patients receive.

When I sat down with her, she explained, "Jen, cash flow is so tight in my business right now. I'm waiting for $75 a month to come in from each patient, but I need a large infusion of revenue now. I need sales. How can I make this happen quickly?"

Using my Value-Based Pricing process, I analyzed her business and found that just by changing her pricing structure, we could generate instant revenue in her business—and lots of it—in a very short period of time.

I moved Ana to Value-Based Pricing and the results were extraordinary. Within forty-eight hours, she was closing $950–$1,150 packages versus her original asking price of $75 per month.

Here's what Ana's pricing looks like after the makeover:

| Basic | Deluxe | Premium |
|---|---|---|
| ~~$900~~ <br> **$750 / year** <br> Or $75 per month <br> **(save $150 annually)** | ~~$1140~~ <br> **$950 / year** <br> Or $95 per month <br> **(save $190 annually)** | ~~$1,380~~ <br> **$1150 / year** <br> Or $115 per month <br> **(save $230 annually)** |
| No copayments | No copayments | No copayments |
| Same day or next day extended appointments | Same day or next day extended appointments | Same day or next day extended appointments |
| Unlimited visits each month | Unlimited visits each month | Unlimited visits each month |
| Cell phone and video chat visits | Cell phone and video chat visits | Cell phone and video chat visits |
| Annual physical with comprehensive wellness evaluation | Annual physical with comprehensive evaluation - **PLUS free wellness labs** | Annual physical with comprehensive evaluation - **PLUS free wellness labs** |
| Quick response by phone from provider or support staff | Quick response by phone from provider or support staff | Quick response by phone from provider or support staff |
| Free lab draws | Free lab draws | Free lab draws |
| Availability to purchase most medications in the office | Availability to purchase most medications in the office | Availability to purchase most medications in the office |
| Nutrition and weight loss counseling | Nutrition and weight loss counseling | Nutrition and weight loss counseling |
| Hormone and adrenal assessments | Hormone and adrenal assessments | Hormone and adrenal assessments |
| One free vitamin B12 or B-lipo injection | Free B-lipo package (total of 4 injections) | Free B-lipo package (total of 4 injections) |
| | Discounts on supplements | Discounts on IV therapy |
| | | Discounts on supplements |
| | | Free door-to-door delivery on prescriptions and supplements |
| | | Care for visiting, out-of-town family, and friends |

By moving away from flat-rate pricing ($75 per month) and moving to Value-Based Pricing, Ana was able to clearly explain and demonstrate the value to her patients, make her competition irrelevant, and generate infusions of cash into her business almost overnight.

This same exercise in moving toward Value-Based Pricing could also be applied in a coaching or consulting business quite easily.

**NOW**
# DO THIS NOW!
**NOW**

Use the blank chart below to start building your Value-Based Pricing model

| GOOD | BETTER | BEST |
|------|--------|------|
|      |        |      |
|      |        |      |
|      |        |      |
|      |        |      |
|      |        |      |
|      |        |      |

# CHAPTER 3

# Systems Set You Free

*Limiting Belief:*
The hot, new platform/software/
media is the best.

**TRUTH:**
Avoid shiny-object syndrome. Aim for
evergreen systems.

A s I laid on the gurney in the ER with a throbbing pain in my side, a surgeon told me I had a tumor.

*How can this be?* I thought silently as I tried to process the surgeon's words. *Just moments ago I was at a business networking event, and now I'm here. How is this happening to me? Does my life really matter?*

For years, I had been blindly checking off boxes and doing what was expected of me, moving (I thought) towards a "secure future" only to find out it's very shallow once you get there. I'm sure you know what I mean. Maybe you've heard some of these phrases:

- "Go to college so you can get a good job."
- "Buy a sports car and a house in Florida with a pool."
- "Don't stop climbing that corporate ladder until you reach the top."

Sure, our folks mean well when they tell us these things, but once I earned a master's degree, landed a six-figure job, and bought a house in Florida with a pool out back and a red sports car parked in front, I realized I still wasn't fully living.

For most people who have the guts to leave the security of the corporate world and make the leap into entrepreneurship, the results are dismal. They are barely making it on a take-home pay of $40,000 per year, not to mention an 80% failure rate, on average, in the first eighteen months of going out on their own.

That's hardly enough to cover a mortgage, let alone make a difference in the world.

*Doesn't my life have a bigger meaning than collecting a paycheck? Can't I use my gifts and talents to make an impact?* I thought, squirming under the stiff, bleached hospital sheets.

It was that day when everything changed for me and I decided to give up the good to go for great. Leave it to God to create a life-changing moment!

Fast forward, and now I've unlocked the secret to building a business that can be run from anywhere in the world *and* brings in a great income. Clients come calling and opportunities come out of the woodwork.

## Marketing Inspiration from
## *Shark Tank's* Barbara Corcoran

In January 2013, I sat in the front row of the *Entrepreneur* magazine conference in Dallas watching Barbara Corcoran speak to a crowd of hundreds of eager business owners. There were dozens of round tables at the foot of the stage, holding people with their gazes fixed on Barbara and hanging on her every word.

My husband and I had traveled to the conference when I started my first version of a marketing consultancy. We were there to hear Barbara speak, primarily, and to meet new prospective clients secondarily. But what happened that day changed my life forever.

As we listened to hour upon hour of presentations from business leaders sharing their tips on how to grow a business, I realized that we all had missed the answer that was right in front of us.

I looked at how Barbara was using her clout and fame to get on the stage, and I thought, *Wow, she is amazing!*

There she was, up on a stage with all eyes fixed on her as she demonstrated mastery over the primary marketing problem that all entrepreneurs struggle with: getting attention. And she was being paid to do it! She was being *paid* to market her business.

Then, I noticed her team selling her books in the lobby and another lightbulb went off. *Aha! She's taken what she knows and put it into a format that can help millions of people. She's systemized what she knows.*

I did the math and figured that she probably made at least $50,000 for the speaking gig and sold another $3,000 in books on that one day of the conference. Plus, the connections made regarding public relations for her brand and business were invaluable.

But the craziest part was that she was only there for about an hour that day! When she was done, she hopped on her jet and traveled to her next destination.

The book did the selling for her! She was able to position herself as an expert, write a book once, and get paid for it over and over again!

### JOIN THE FREE INSTANT MEDIA MOGUL COMMUNITY
#### WWW.FACEBOOK.COM/GROUPS/INSTANTMEDIAMOGUL

That's when I realized I didn't want to build a traditional business the way most people do it, selling consulting by the hour. I wanted to do what Barbara did and sell my knowledge as a speaker, author, and coach.

And so that's what I did.

I was successful because I focused on *two* things: I positioned myself as an expert by speaking on stages and publishing magazines, books, and videos; and I created systems to help more people.

This narrowed focus gave me the freedom I so desperately desired.

If you're like me and you're ready to make a bigger impact, elevate your influence, and generate the income you deserve, then I welcome you to the Instant Media Mogul community, where we help you outsource your marketing!

## Time Management vs. Action Management

We can't manage time, but we can manage our actions.

One of the very important perspective shifts that will impact your success as an entrepreneur who leverages Outsourced Marketing Systems to grow your business is to know that even if most of the people in your industry suffer from a failing business that is saddled with debt, there will still be a mindset that does not embrace new ideas or being different. This human condition of having a fixed mindset keeps businesses from succeeding and industries from progressing. But, in actuality, the secret to success is to do the exact opposite of what everyone in your industry is doing.

If your day is consumed by caring for clients, managing employees, or even working at your day job, you must have excellent systems in place so that when you wake up every morning you know exactly what needs to be done to move your business forward.

It's important to avoid sitting behind your computer in the morning and not knowing exactly what needs to get done that day to build your Outsourced Marketing Systems. You will know if this is a perspective shift that needs to take place in your life if you are "winging" much of your marketing—meaning you're making it up as you go along. You may feel like you are spending hours and hours posting on social media, cold-emailing strangers, or doing other nonscalable marketing activities, and getting little to no results.

Once you have a strategy that works, you can document the steps around the core activities and assign tasks to your team members. But, first, you need a system.

## Systems Before Team

Whether your new Outsourced Marketing System starts with professional speaking, creating YouTube videos, or another big, marketing domino, it is imperative that you identify the main strategy so you can identify the systems involved in that strategy. For example, as a YouTuber, systems that I need to succeed include the following:

- Topic research
- Script writing
- Thumbnail design
- Titles and key terms
- Video production and editing
- Video optimization and ranking
- Video promotion
  - Social media
  - Email marketing

## Success Story

Sharri Harmel is a magazine publisher based out of Paris, France, with a second home in Boston, MA. Sharri's digital and print magazine focuses on helping women in their 40s–60s build their dream lives, which often include traveling the world (like Sharri does), starting a side hustle, or working on personal development. Sharri became my client because she was frustrated with the work produced by her initial outsourced team. The design work was unimpressive, the technical aspects were causing major frustrations, and the team's attitudes were very negative. We worked together to better define her marketing funnel system, and to identify the key systems needed as well as some that could be eliminated. By first reorganizing her "Buyer's Journey" and building a new sales funnel, she was able to streamline her entire process and gain clarity on how her marketing should work. Sharri up-leveled her team members who are producing better work, and she now has a working Outsourced Marketing System and an enthusiastic team behind her.

Each area of this system has unique software programs, tech tools, benchmarks for success, dos and don'ts, and current trends. I don't need to be an expert on all of the tactical decisions in each area of the system, but I do need to know enough about what's working now in order to make well-educated decisions when investing time and money.

Instead of trying to learn every little aspect of these various steps in the process and how to use every tool that's related, I hire professionals who already know the ins and outs. I build my team based on what actions need to be taken and trust them to do what they do best.

Zig Ziglar, a famous American salesman and motivational speaker, said, "You don't build a business. You build people, then people build the business."

The reason why I say that you need to know your overall system is because setting your overall marketing strategy is not the responsibility of your outsourced team. It is not appropriate to ask a virtual assistant to figure out how you make money. It is not your website designer's role to determine your business model. If you are frustrated with your team's performance, it may be because you need to spend some time working through your strategy so you can give them better direction. This book will help you do that.

## Your YouTube Marketing Strategy

Here's an outline of my recommended YouTube marketing strategy:

1. Publish a new long-form video every week that answers a specific question and is optimized for search engines.
2. In the video content, video description, and channel banner, link to a Lead Magnet that turns viewers into email-list subscribers.

3. Once the Lead Magnet subscriber enters their email, have the page redirect to a thank-you page with the offer *and* link to your calendar to schedule a consultation.
4. Have an email autoresponder send the link to your calendar to schedule a consultation.

In 2022, I landed 167 opt-ins on one of my Lead Magnets and sixty-seven booked consultations from this *one* marketing system, resulting in hundreds of thousands of dollars in revenue. Most importantly, this system works 24/7/365, and generates awareness, leads, and conversions to my calendar.

Because of this one system, I do not worry about where my leads are going to come from. I have peace of mind and assurance that my marketing is working even when I'm not. This system has set me free.

You can find freedom too!

# CHAPTER 4

# Team Members Build Your Business

***TRUTH:***
You just need to know exactly what
you require.

One of the best gifts you can give yourself as an entrepreneur is investing in team members who understand the tactics behind your marketing strategy better than you do. For example, instead of trying to learn and master YouTube thumbnail design on my own, I sought out one of the best YouTube thumbnail designers in the industry. Through a Facebook group for YouTubers, I was introduced to Ardi, who has been my YouTube thumbnail designer for years. He does an excellent job and is much better at graphic design than I could ever be. With his help, I get much better results on my video click-through rates than I would if I'd tried to design the YouTube thumbnails myself.

Investing in professionals on my team who understand the ins and outs of the tactical aspects involved in my industry is the best use of my time and energy. I don't need to stay on top of all of the tactical trends; instead, I can just make great hiring decisions and get out of their way. Because of my team members, and with systems and processes in place, I now have a business model that runs smoothly.

## Working with a Marketing Coach or Consultant

Working with a marketing coach or consultant can be an excellent investment in your business if you can clearly communicate what you need, just as is necessary with your other team members. It is important to have realistic expectations when working with a coach.

Think about it this way: Doctors do not make you healthy. Fitness instructors do not make you fit. Coaches do not make you rich.

The best use of your time, when working with a generalist marketing coach or consultant, is to work on your *unique* strategy. Your marketing strategy is the most important aspect of doing your Outsourced Marketing System work.

However, there are coaches who are tactical coaches. For example, I do have a YouTube coach who does not do general marketing coaching for me but focuses instead on

## Seven Questions to Ask When Hiring a Coach/Consultant

1. Why do you love coaching/consulting?
2. What differentiates you from other coaches/consultants?
3. What types of clients do you like?
4. What qualifications do you have that make you the best person for this job?
5. How do you work with clients on a daily basis?
6. Who have you worked with before and what did they say about your work? (Ask for references.)
7. What is your superpower?

only helping me with my strategy for my YouTube channel. Tactical coaches are completely different from strategy coaches, and you need to know what type of coach you are hiring before you sign a contract. Let's define the different options.

**Strategic coaches** are general business coaches who take a birds-eye view of your business and can identify your strengths, weaknesses, opportunities, and threats from the outside looking in.

**Tactical coaches** offer skills and knowledge related to technical areas of expertise, such as how to grow your presence on YouTube, how to become a professional speaker, or some other specific skill.

## Working with an Outsourced Chief Marketing Officer (CMO)

A CMO is a Chief Marketing Officer. Just like a CEO (Chief Executive Officer) or a COO (Chief Operating Officer), a CMO is an executive-level position within a company. A CMO has the responsibility of overseeing the development and execution of an organization's advertising and marketing strategies with the purpose of hitting revenue goals. A CMO will work with your team to set creative direction, map out the "buyer's journey" and sales funnels, help craft messaging, and make decisions about media platforms. A CMO will also set the marketing budget and be responsible for managing team members.

Outsourcing the CMO role can be a viable alternative to having a full-time employee. An outsourced CMO will work on a contract basis with a set number of hours per week and or deliverables that are determined by the legal agreement.

Your business is ready for an outsourced CMO if your business makes at least multiple six figures in revenue, has expansion goals, invests in marketing, and needs a better approach to managing marketing and team members, both internally and externally.

# Seven Questions to Ask When Interviewing an Outsourced CMO

1. Tell me about yourself.
2. What is your level of experience?
3. What is your level of education?
4. What projects are you most proud of?
5. How do you measure success?
6. What is your leadership style?
7. What is your superpower?

## What to Look for in an Outsourced CMO

- Entrepreneurial spirit and experience
- High-level analytical skills
- Demonstrated ability to create effective campaigns
- Ability to lead and inspire a team
- Flexibility and initiative
- Passionate customer advocacy
- Thorough knowledge of marketing principles, including brand, product, and service management
- Recognition of changing market dynamics

## Working with Project Managers

An important person in your Outsourced Marketing System is your project manager. Your project manager is the person who acts as the coordinator between you and your team of editors, copywriters, designers, developers, and creatives.

If you cannot afford a project manager, then you must step into this role. Here are the aspects and characteristics that make great project managers:

- See the big picture and grasp the strategic goal
- Communicate with the technical team, in their language, and emphasize timelines and budgetary goals
- Set project timelines and manage deadlines
- Utilize project management systems, such as Trello, Asana, Basecamp, or a self-created system
- Prioritize multiple tasks for multiple projects at one time
- Employ systems-oriented thinking and document steps taken in each process
- Understand how to use many technical programs, including Google apps, calendar scheduling systems, email, etc.
- Are proficient in finding, recruiting, and managing technical and creative team members

A good project manager will, in the long run, give you peace of mind, more free time, better results, and cost savings.

## What Do Project Managers Do?

- Foster communication that is clear, concise, and focused
- Set and manage deadlines for your projects based on goals
- Build and use a system to ensure consistency and monitor progress
- Work with your team members (and you) to stay on track

The best project manager I ever had made managing my marketing so simple that we had only two meetings over the course of the two years she was on my team. Karen was a project manager based in the Philippines, and due to the fourteen-hour time zone difference, having virtual meetings was just not practical. Karen and I worked together to create systems out of all my marketing strategies. She documented every step in the process for every type of project and created Standard Operating Procedures (SOPs) that could be used to train team members. The SOPs were uploaded into our Trello Project Management system (see the next chapter for more on how to set this up), saving us hours of time and thousands of dollars. When Karen left the business to go back to school, she left me with the most valuable gift: a process that could be seamlessly picked up and implemented by our new project manager. We didn't skip a beat. I will be forever grateful to Karen for that gift.

# Working with Virtual Assistants and Creative Team Members

What do you think when you hear a peer say, "I have a team" or "I will get my team on the project"?

Do you think to yourself: *Ugh, that sounds like a lot of work to manage a team? Do I have enough work? Is it expensive? How will I manage them with everything else I have going on?*

I used to think that having a team of assistants sounded great, but also very intimidating and time-consuming. But now I have successfully managed a totally virtual, outsourced team while only having two meetings in one year.

They work for me eighty hours each month and handle all my tech, website, graphic design, video optimization, video repurposing for social media, and some client project work.

We do it all without phone calls or meetings since they are fourteen hours ahead of my time zone.

This is eighty hours per month I get back into my life to work *on* my business, health, mindset, and strategy.

If this sounds like something you need, let's get into it.

To make it possible to manage a virtual team with little to no meetings or phone calls, you need to be crystal clear on what you need to be done and why.

You can't leave it up to the team members to think and strategize. You need to be responsible for that part.

So, you must have a clear strategy documented step-by-step before you hand off work.

If you don't do this part, it's like hiring a new employee to come to work, and there are no bosses or managers in the office. The new employee would have no idea what to do.

You can't say: "Update my website." That's not clear enough.

You need to say: "Here are the exact updates I need on my website," and then show and tell them what you need exactly. I love using Loom.com to create short, screen-share videos for my team members.

You also need to make great hiring decisions and trust those new hires to do their jobs. There is nothing worse than being micromanaged. Don't be a micromanager!

In the next chapter, I will show you how to give great input to your team members, so you get what you need and can cut down or eliminate meetings, and save time and money. In the meantime, here are questions to ask when hiring outsourced team members.

### Questions to Ask When Hiring Outsourced Team Members

1. What do you like the most about working as a virtual assistant/designer/developer?
2. What days do you work?
3. What type of work do you love to do?
4. What type of work is not for you?
5. How many hours are you available to work each week?
6. What do I do if I need you off-hours for an emergency?

7. What software programs do you use?

8. How do you work (virtual only)?

9. What questions do you have for me?

Remember that it's critical to be clear on which team members you need, who does what, and how their work is imperative to your success in building your Outsourced Marketing System.

## Working with Agencies

When I worked as a marketing executive from 1999 to 2003 for NASA at the Kennedy Space Center (KSC), one of my responsibilities was managing an advertising agency for our creative projects, including TV advertising productions, billboard design, radio commercials, and print collateral. I was responsible for millions of dollars in paid advertising campaigns, plus an on-site consumer research team that interviewed our guests regarding where they were from and what brought them to the Kennedy Space Center, which is one of the most visited tourist attractions in Florida competing with Disney World, Sea World, Universal Studios, and all the water parks and hundreds of smaller vacation attractions.

Our advertising agency was based in Orlando, and we were one of the top-tier agencies in Florida. They did great work for us and were very creative. Together, our team won multiple regional ADDY Awards for our work. The American Advertising Awards, playfully referred to as the ADDY Awards, is the largest and most representative award ceremony in the advertising industry. The mission of the award ceremony is to recognize and reward the creative spirit and the inspired nature of those in advertising. One of the key things I learned managing agency partners was that sometimes creatives have different goals than clients, and it's important to recognize those differences.

In true space-geek fashion, I had to wear a pager clipped to my belt at all times while I was at work, which would provide me with hourly updates on the number of guests we had, counting them as they walked through the turnstiles at the ticket booths. As the manager of advertising, I needed to know if my marketing efforts were working because every dollar counted. Most people don't know this, but the tourism part of KSC is not funded by tax dollars. All of the KSC visitor center exhibits, restaurants, theaters, and guest experiences are funded by ticket sales, retail sales, and food sales. The pager kept track of how many guests walked thorough the turnstiles on an hourly basis. We knew what our averages were and could make day-by-day decisions to either run more advertising or pull back based on the results.

While I was busy counting clicks, the agency was sometimes focused on creative perfection and would often push to create projects that would build the NASA brand and win ADDY awards, which were not necessarily trackable, to lead guests walking through the turnstiles. Sometimes we had to compromise to try to hit both goals.

One of my claims to fame in this environment was that I helped to create the very first direct response TV campaign. We ran TV commercials across the nation promoting a "space coast visitor's kit," which families could get mailed to their houses by calling a "1-800" number. This experience trained me for a career in direct response advertising and to count every action. It also taught me how to effectively work with agencies and learn pitfalls to avoid.

## Tips for Working with Agencies

- Be sure that all creative work is done as "work for hire." Work for hire refers to works whose ownership belongs to a third party (you) rather than the creator. Under general copyright principals, a copyright becomes the property of the author who created the work. However, "work for hire" is an exception to this principle, and can be established through contract before a particular work is created.
- Maintain administrative control of all the logins for your website, email marketing, social media, and any other software accounts used by the agency to do your marketing. These logins should be kept it a safe space.
- Build all digital assets on accounts that *you* own. The problem to avoid is that if/when you discontinue your contract, you don't want to be held hostage by the

agency because your systems were built on platforms they control.

- Get every project agreement in writing. It is important to know what is within in the "scope" of the project and when requests are out of the scope of the project. Out-of-scope work will result in overage fees and has the potential to cost you thousands of dollars in unplanned expenses.
- Assign a dedicated point person in your company to work with the agency contact. On the agency side, this person is usually called the "account executive."
- Set clear goals and expectations up front.
- Include the agency as part of your team and work to rally them behind your mission and vision. Don't treat them as outsiders.
- Implement "creative briefs" in your process. "Creative briefs" will save you hours of time and tens of thousands of dollars by being clear and upfront about what you need for each project. Use the example "creative brief" on the next page.
- Have a clear approval process with multiple people involved to catch mistakes.
- Remember that you are not their only client. Agencies have multiple clients and many priorities that they are juggling in addition to you. By giving plenty of notice, staying in scope on projects, and responding in a timely manner, you will save everyone from headaches.

## *Example Creative Brief*

| | |
|---|---|
| **Summary** | |
| **Target Audience** | |
| **Goals/Metrics** | |
| **Deliverables** | |
| **Team** | |
| **Timeline** | |
| **Link to Resources/Files** | |
| **Budget** | |

# CHAPTER 5

# Tactics, Tools, and Time

*Limiting Belief:*
*Other people are better*
*at marketing than me.*

**TRUTH:**
Most people are hiding behind
curated branding that's producing
no measurable results.

As consumers of products and services, we are most often exposed to a type of marketing that is typically called "brand awareness" marketing. Brand awareness marketing is adopted by bigger companies like Coca-Cola, Kellogg's, and any company with deep pockets that can afford to spend hundreds of thousands or millions of dollars on TV commercials and other forms of advertising.

These TV commercials typically focus on creating a "feel-good experience" for the viewer and conclude with putting up a logo at the end of the TV spot. Think about the most recent Nike commercial you've seen that probably includes some black-and-white gritty footage of sweaty athletes with a motivational speech voiceover. The commercial fades to black and the Nike swoosh logo pops on the screen saying, "Just do it." Very rarely do these brand awareness marketing efforts drive a consumer's behavior to take immediate action with the company.

As a small business owner, every single dollar we have coming into our business needs to be accounted for, especially in our marketing.

Direct response marketing enables you to get your message in front of the right people, at the right time, and focuses on measuring results. A mistake I see a lot of experts and influencers making is that they are focused on brand awareness marketing and not on direct response marketing.

The basic idea of direct response marketing is making sure that it will be *directly* influential to the ideal, perfect client and a clear *response* will be measured.

As a keynote speaker, and a professional YouTuber, at business leadership conferences and events, I realize that speaking at events or on-camera is just the beginning of my relationship with the audience. I need a way to be able to continue the conversation after the show or conference. This connection is important not only to provide support to the audience members so they can actually implement the ideas that I share with them, but also to continue to build my business on the back-end.

As you become more highly visible in your career and industry, and are you are asked to speak on podcasts, at events, or in interviews, you must determine how to convert that listener or audience member into a potential prospect or client. What is the next step you want them to take after they see or hear you?

Think of your public appearance as the very first step in your relationship. How do you want to move that relationship forward?

One idea for how to enhance your relationship with an audience member or a listener is to invite them to become a part of your community. Do you have a Facebook group that you could invite the audience member to join?

Another idea is to have a free downloadable gift or Lead Magnet on your website that visitors could access in exchange for their email addresses. More on that in the next chapter.

Perhaps you could create a podcast you invite them to listen and subscribe to. As an expert, you will be asked to speak on other people's platforms, and you will need to have a systemized process in place to connect you with other people's circles of influence.

The golden rule of direct response marketing is that there must always be an offer. An offer doesn't mean that you need to sell something. A smarter way to look at direct response marketing is to think of it like you are marketing information.

Depending on the type of business you have, you will want to consider one of two strategies: information marketing or information-first marketing.

# Information Marketing

With information marketing, you are marketing your ideas, insights, tools, resources, and anything that is helpful and of use to your viewer, listener, or audience member.

Information marketing is typically used by online marketers who get paid for what they know. Perhaps you are a life coach and have created a course or training on how to thrive during divorce or another unexpected life transition. Maybe you have a membership site where you have stored all of your best ideas and you sell access to the site to small business owners as a way for them to educate themselves. Or maybe you are a coach or consultant who gets paid for your specialized knowledge. In all these cases, information marketing is a powerful way to build your influence and impact others so you may build your income.

Webinars and live speaking events are my favorite platforms for my business, and I highly recommend mastering webinars and live-event presentations.

Send me an email at jen@jendevore.com if you'd like more information about how to book me to present to your group.

# Information-First Marketing

Examples of information-first marketing presentations include speaking, writing books, hosting seminars, providing downloads on your website, or creating podcasts to build an audience for your business. Information-first marketing works well for doctors, lawyers, realtors, or other service providers who work directly with clients to help them problem solve. The great thing about information-first marketing is that it can be quantified—the first rule of direct-response marketing is that everything must be measured.

An example of information first-marketing could look like this:

Susan is a commercial real estate advisor who is in a very competitive market. Susan needs a way to differentiate herself from her competition and is tired of cold calling investors and facing rejection. The investors currently see her as "just another sales person" and not as a trusted advisor.

Susan has been listening to podcasts every morning on her run, and one day she has the epiphany that these real estate advisors on these shows don't know anything more than she does. In fact, she knows, deep down inside, that she has insights and ideas that could really make a difference if investors just knew the truth.

Taking her frustration from being rejected over and over, and seeing a gap for fresh ideas in the podcast space, Susan decides to start a podcast.

On day one, Susan writes a simple, two-sentence email and sends it to wealthy real estate investors she found on the internet, asking them to be guests on her podcast. She invites them to share how they've been able to become successful in multi-family property investments. Soon, amazing things start to happen!

The commercial real estate investors, who typically would not give Susan the time of day, are flattered at the opportunity to be interviewed on a podcast. They agree to participate.

(People love talking about themselves and enjoy the opportunity to share their opinions on a vocal platform.) And, voila! Susan, who has been trying to cold call and cold email these investors, finds that her podcast offers a foot-in-the-door strategy that's almost guaranteed to work. Once the investors agree to talk on her podcast, she establishes a personal relationship with them that puts her on a more even playing field.

The interviews are scheduled easily by sending a link to an online calendar like Acuity, Schedule Once, or Calendly. On the day of the interview, Susan sets up a Zoom recorded call to conduct the interview with the commercial real estate investor. The call could be done over video or the call could be done with audio only. Either one gives Susan the opportunity to connect on a personal and professional level with an investor.

After the call, Susan could have the interview edited by a virtual assistant on a platform like UpWork or Fiverr. The virtual assistant could then upload the final file to the platform of Susan's choice. The link could then be shared with the commercial real estate investors, who could then link it to their professional networks.

Now that Susan has a compelling, foot-in-the-door strategy, her work has just begun. She then must work on converting those podcast guests into prospects who could possibly convert into clients. Susan could develop a VIP email campaign that would be shared exclusively with her podcast listeners, and she could continue to provide insights and strategies. She could measure the results of her email marketing campaign and make an offer for a free, real estate portfolio review. Her goal should be to nurture these prospective clients over time, and to stay top-of-mind so when the investor is ready to buy—she is their go-to expert.

Importantly, Susan would need to track and measure her results.

Items she could track include the following:

- Number of podcast interview emails sent each week
- Number of interviews scheduled or "yes" emails received
- Number of subscribers on her list
- Email open rates and click-through rates
- Number of portfolio reviews scheduled
- Number of new clients booked
- Number of properties sold
- Total revenue of new business in each month, quarter, or year

Here's the big question: Are you beginning to see how this could work in your business?

Information marketing is a very powerful way of building bridges and getting your foot in the door where you otherwise might not be able to do it.

You don't need another shiny marketing tactic, you just need an Outsourced Marketing System.

# Manage Your Outsourced
# Marketing Projects & Team with Ease

In my experience, there are certain tools that every entrepreneur needs in order to effectively outsource marketing and stay on top of productivity.

Here are some of my favorite marketing tools:

- Online calendar to make scheduling easier
  - Calendly
- Online payment processing to make collecting payments faster
  - Stripe
- Website and blog for SEO
  - WordPress
- Sales funnel builder for landing pages
  - ClickFunnels or Kajabi
- Product shop for online sales of physical products
  - Shopify
- Email marketing & Customer Relationship Manager
  - ActiveCampaign
- File & Document Storage
  - Google Drive
- Screen recordings to show what you mean and reduce meetings
  - Loom
- Project management software to stay on schedule and keep everyone on track
  - Trello

Of course, there are other software programs that do similar things as the ones I recommend. This is not a comprehensive list, just my personal preferences. I vouch only for tools that I personally use in my own business.

*Find a complete list of tech and tools I use and recommend at*

WWW.STUFFJENLOVES.COM

## Setting Up Your Project Management System Workspace

Since the focus of this book is how to outsource your marketing, I'm not going to dive into the technical aspects of the various website options, email marketing platforms, and billing systems, because otherwise we'll get into the weeds. But I do want to take a moment to walk you through how to set up your "workspace" on Trello. These ideas can be used in any project management system, such as Asana or Basecamp.

To begin, you will set up a "workspace" with a board for outsourced marketing and then individual "lists" on the board. You can invite team members to the entire board or to individual project lists.

I recommend the following lists on your Outsourced Marketing Board:

- Assets - This list is where you should upload your
brand guide, logo files, marketing photography, logins,

and other items that are frequently used in your marketing efforts. By having them organized in one place, they will be easier to find, saving time and money.

- Templates - This list is where you offer templates for actions that recur frequently. For example, I create templates for my weekly YouTube videos, email blasts, My Business posts on Google, and more.
- Recurring - This list is for actions that do not need a template, but still recur weekly. For example, my YouTube thumbnail orders go here.
- To Do - This list is for general or one-time tasks, like a new social media banner or a website update.
- Review - This list is where To Do items are moved by the team member once they are ready for review.
- Done - This list is where items move after they are reviewed and completed.

Here is a screenshot of my template Board setup with the six lists.

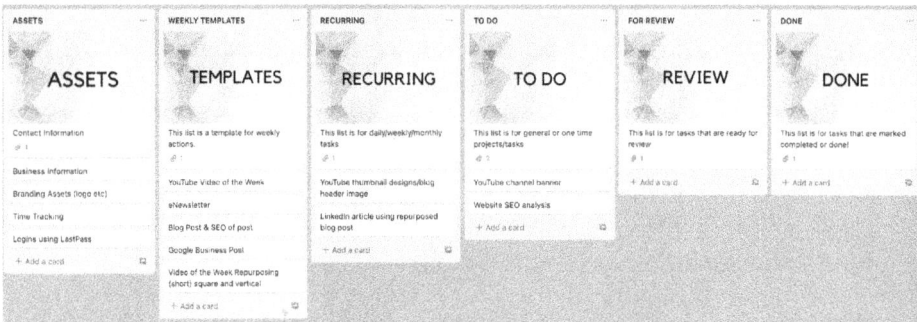

Once your board and lists are setup, all communication begins by creating a card for a project.

Here's an example of a card for a new project and how I provide input to kick off a project:

> **@card** this is going to be a new weekly video editing task for my client Turning the Corner.
>
> I have documented out my current system and provided links to the Drive folders and my Canva templates here:
>
> SYSTEM OUTLINE AND TEMPLATES:
> 🗐 TTC video instructions
>
> DUE DATES:
> Each video set will be due to me weekly on Thursday.
> Client will provide edits or approval by Friday.
> SVS to provide final video files before Monday.
> Videos get uploaded and released by Jen every Tuesday at 1pm MST.
>
> ASSETS:
> For this first set, here are the assets:
>
> Michael Thatcher - 1/24 release date
>
> Raw video:
> 🔗 Raw Files to Edit - Google Drive
>
> Timestamp to use: 6:05 to 6:44
>
> Headliner text for video graphics: ONLY LOVE THE MISSION OR THE WORK TOO?
>
> Thumbnail for animated end screen:
>
> michael thatcher 1:24.png
>
> Thank you.

You will notice that there are links in the card to files and documents that are on Google Drive. Google Drive is my preferred place to store files and documents.

By using a project management system, you can completely eliminate the need to email things back and forth. All communication about projects takes place on Trello. When done effectively, you could eliminate the need for meetings as well.

For a full tutorial on using Trello effectively, please visit their YouTube channel https://www.youtube.com/c/trello or Trello's online Help Center.

## How to Delegate Effectively

Keep in mind that you, as the business owner, need to provide everything needed before starting a project. It's important to clarify the following:

> *Clear Instructions*—I love using Loom.com to create short, simple, explanatory videos.
>
> *Creative Brief*—a document that outlines the creative approach and deliverables for a marketing or advertising campaign. It connects the creative work to the broader business goals by clearly outlining the strategy of the campaign. Include photos, logos, brand guides, etc.
>
> *Schedule*—offer a suggested deadline and always be flexible
>
> *Goals*—the overall goals of the project

## Avoiding Shiny-Object Syndrome

Once you know what needs to happen before the sale and understand what strategy is needed to help you reach those initial goals, you will become clearer and more focused. Avoiding shiny-object syndrome is important for entrepreneurs. Marketing can be fun when it works well, but it can also become very distracting if you jump around from idea to idea.

It is more important that you pick one marketing strategy and take consistent action instead of trying to manage multiple strategies simultaneously.

Shiny-object syndrome happens when people focus on something current or trendy, yet drop it as soon as something new takes its place.

For business owners and marketers, this constant flux can put you on a hamster wheel that feels like you never gain traction on any one thing.

When we start to feel frustrated with our marketing, it can temporarily feel like a lot of fun to start something new rather than hunker down and fix the issues that are going on around our current strategy.

For example, if you've been trying to gain traction on You-Tube, but you're frustrated with getting videos to rank, it may seem easier to just move over to TikTok, where SEO isn't as much of a factor.

So you head to TikTok and start making videos, yet the same cycle repeats. You get frustrated because it's taking longer to work.

So you jump over to IG Reels to give that a go—and get the same result.

Six months later, you still haven't nailed down any one platform, and you're feeling burnt out and frustrated.

To avoid this situation, you must first have a solid strategy.

## *Success Story*

In 2020, I lost my entire professional speaking business and main strategy for booking coaching clients when pandemic lockdowns impacted the conference industry and live events were canceled. By quickly changing my strategy from speaking on stages to creating YouTube videos, I was able to build a six-figure business in less than one year despite not knowing the tactical elements needed for a successful YouTube channel. Instead, I focused on building a scalable system that could be managed by my team. A successful strategy will outperform marketing tactics every time.

Picking marketing tactics without a strategy is like trying to solve a puzzle without having the picture on the box as a guide.

You've got this blue piece and this yellow piece but have no idea how they should fit together and what the big picture should look like.

## Create Batches of Content

My videos are researched, written, and planned four weeks in advance, and four at a time.

This system allows me to keep building momentum because I have a system that my team can help me with.

Pick *one* platform to focus on at a time.

Now, I know that all the gurus say to diversify, but that is the root of the shiny-object syndrome issue.

Only diversify after you have one platform growing at a steady pace.

Once the flow is going, then we can add a new platform.

As an entrepreneur, you are not afraid to start new things—I love that about you! But to avoid shiny-object syndrome, we need to:

- Do your research for what's possible
- Set goals
- Stick with what you start
- Get help when you need it

# Download a FREE
# Marketing Action Guide

JEN DEVORE RICHTER

📱 SCAN ME

WWW.JENDEVORE.COM/GUIDE

# CHAPTER 6

# Results Rule, Always

*Limiting Belief:*
*I need 10,000 followers to*
*make money with marketing.*

**TRUTH:**
Vanity metrics don't matter.

**M**arch 15, 2013, was the scariest day of my life.

In an effort to jump-start my new business as a marketing consultant, I was leading a networking group in Jacksonville Beach, FL. On that day, I was standing in front of my peers leading the group when suddenly an excruciating pain gripped my right side. It nearly brought me to my knees. Embarrassingly, I had to pack up my laptop and drive myself to the emergency room.

I was scared to death as my fiancé (now husband) was in Atlanta for work. The antiseptic smell of the hospital, the beeping machines, and the fogginess from the morphine were creating a very unpleasant experience.

After the MRI and extensive tests, the doctor sat down, looked me straight in the eye, and said, "Jen, you have a tumor the size of an orange on your uterus. It needs to come out—now."

Everything came crashing down. I was just launching my business, planning a wedding in June in Paris, and rebuilding my life after a nasty divorce.

*I don't have time for a tumor!* I thought to myself.

As an entrepreneur, I knew that surgery would take me out of commission. Without the ability to make connections and seek out clients through networking, I was going to be broke and back to square one, professionally.

Eventually, I closed my little office at the beach and had to put my dream on hold to recover from having three organs removed via four surgeries in two years.

While that was the worst thing to ever happen to me physically, financially, and emotionally, it was also the best thing.

Here's why: during that time, I began to picture a different version of myself using my gifts and talents to impact people's lives on a bigger scale.

The process has not been easy. I have had detours and set-backs and made tons of mistakes. I've had to sacrifice a lot. I've had to focus like a laser.

But now I am thankful to say that I am healthy, happily married, living in an awesome city, and finally owning the business of my dreams.

In 2019, I was awarded "Innovator of the Year" for excellence in business coaching out of over 550+ coaches globally.

In 2022, I was awarded the "National Speaker's Association—Colorado Chapter President's Award" for excellence.

As an outsourced chief marketing officer and magazine publisher, I have the very best clients, whom I adore and are an absolute joy to work with, as we build their businesses and inspire their teams.

Plus, my YouTube channel and free Facebook group are serving over 120,000 entrepreneurs around the globe and helping them to build successful businesses, even if the statistics say they can't.

I am grateful for everything I had to overcome. It has given me a drive to succeed and, most importantly, to *serve.*

My health issues in 2013 forced me to reprioritize many things, to slow down, and to create new processes and systems that would enable me to get the same, or better, results with less effort. My business tripled while my effort and hours worked were cut in half.

This kind of business growth is possible for you too—but you need to focus on what matters and cut the rest.

Here's the truth: Vanity metrics don't matter.

I have proven that it is possible to build a six-figure or even seven-figure business with a small following. You do not need to have tens of thousands of followers to be successful in marketing.

You just need about one thousand people with a problem that you can solve.

## Match Your Marketing to How People Buy

Today's consumers are savvy and skeptical. They've seen it all, heard it all, and expect more out of the brands they do business with.

They're tired of the pitch-fest, brand-focused advertising that floods the airways and clogs up their social media channels.

Instead, they demand to be wowed. They demand to be informed. They demand a better experience from the first touch point to the last.

The problem for most business owners is that the old-school marketing approach is outdated. Its fluff-filled, brand-focused, "look for the next sale" strategies have resulted in dismal high failure rates for small businesses.

80% of small businesses fail, which tells us that these institutions are not reaching their target markets.

Here's a big idea: Match your marketing to the way that people buy.

## Understanding the Buyer's Journey

The Buyer's Journey is a marketing and sales concept that basically begins with the idea that regardless of what you sell and who you sell it to, your customers are on a problem-solving journey.

There is a problem they have that they don't want, and an outcome that they don't currently have.

Understanding exactly what keeps your customers up at night is the first step in getting your marketing to work.

You must know what that problem is and where they are in the journey.

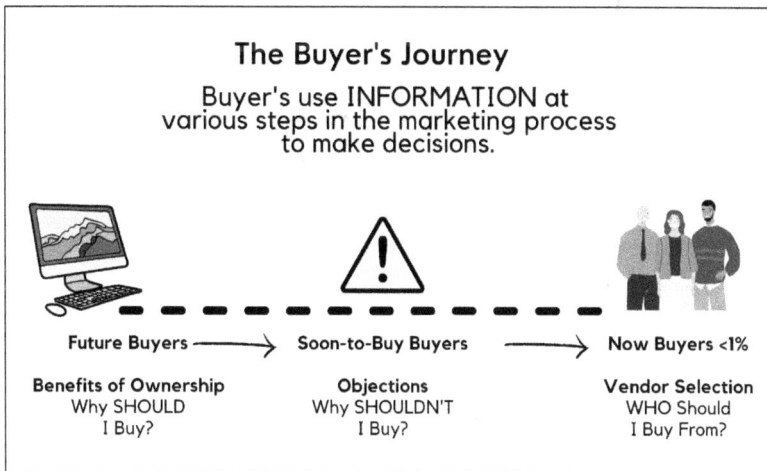

## The Buyer's Journey

Buyer's use INFORMATION at various steps in the marketing process to make decisions.

Future Buyers ———→ Soon-to-Buy Buyers ———→ Now Buyers <1%

| Benefits of Ownership | Objections | Vendor Selection |
|---|---|---|
| Why SHOULD I Buy? | Why SHOULDN'T I Buy? | WHO Should I Buy From? |

Without using industry jargon or trade terminology, it's critical for you to answer this question: What keeps your customers up at night, in their own words?

The answer is what they are searching for on the internet. When you create content that is helpful, entertaining, informative, and inspiring, *and* optimized for search engines, the likelihood of your future customers finding you increases. Using the internet to search for solutions to problems is the key behavior that kicks off the buying process.

If you don't really know what words your customers would use, here's a simple hack to getting the answer: ASK THEM!

Conduct five interviews with your ideal, perfect prospects and clients and write down what they say. Use those words in your customer-focused marketing research. I use tools like VidIQ for YouTube and "keywords everywhere" for Google to conduct research on key-phrases related to my business and to get ideas for content marketing.

Next, the key to making this work is to understand that only 1% of consumers who see your marketing messages are "now buyers," meaning they are ready to buy from you or to hire you now. So how do we reach everyone else?

99% of the market isn't aware of the problem you solve, isn't convinced they need to solve it, and doesn't know which vendor to choose. If you only create marketing for "now buyers" and ignore "future buyers" and "soon-to-buy buyers" you're missing out on 99% of the revenue and market potential.

The major mistake tactical marketers make is creating content that is asking only for a sale. This is a huge mistake! When you market to all—future buyers, soon-to-buy buyers, and now buyers—you increase your revenue potential. If you market only to "now buyers," you are reaching less than 1% of any market.

The key to tapping into the 99% of hidden revenue potential is that marketers should match their marketing to how today's savvy and skeptical consumers buy while providing information that moves them along the Buyer's Journey.

## How to Apply the Buyer's Journey to Social Media

The key to creating a strategy that matches your marketing to the way people buy is to create content focused on the three types of buyers:

1. Future Buyers
2. Soon-to-Buy Buyers
3. Now Buyers

## Content Marketing Ideas for Future Buyers

Here are some content marketing ideas for future buyers:

- Live videos that break down the hidden costs of not solving a problem
- Video interviews with experts on related topics
- Testimonials from happy customers
- Daily, "behind-the-scenes" posts
- Updates to your cover image, profile photo and "about" page
- Conversation starters that ask questions about topics people care about that they can quickly and easily respond to with short answers

## Content Marketing Ideas for
## Soon-to-Buy Buyers

Here are some content marketing ideas for soon-to-buy buyers:

- Live videos that cover frequently asked questions (FAQs)
- Autoposts of your blog posts to social media
- Announcements of your next live event
- Free giveaways to your readers (e.g., checklists or other helpful tips)
- Upgrading your social media fans to your email list
- Replying to comments with open-ended questions

## Content Marketing Ideas for Now Buyers

Here are some content marketing ideas for now buyers:

- "Deal of the Day" offers
- Creating default replies so your customer gets an immediate response when they inquire even if you're busy
- Capturing hot leads and sending a personalized message

Understanding the Buyer's Journey and applying it to your marketing efforts can take you from an unwelcome pest to a welcome guest in your customer's life if you match your marketing to the way that people buy.

While you're building out your Outsourced Marketing System and team, this understanding of the Buyer's Journey is a key element for you to think through and map out so that you can set realistic goals, make the right decisions about the tools you need, and create a marketing plan that will actually work.

## What Is Your True Marketing Goal?

As understood in the Buyer's Journey, it is not realistic to think that someone would see your "Buy Now" marketing offer and automatically send you a check, sign up for your program, or hire you. There needs to be a step before the sale. This might look like any of the following:

- Giveaway offers downloaded
- Consultations booked
- Applications filled out
- Event registrations received
- Demonstrations scheduled
- Webinar sign-ups booked

To find your step before the sale, you need to know how your clients expect to do business with you, which depends on your strategy. Do you sell face-to-face? Do you sell on the phone or over Zoom? Do you sell at live events or on webinars?

If you sell to your prospects while consulting, what is your strategy for booking consultations?

One of the most effective strategies to book consultations is to offer a prerecorded webinar that people can access for free. At the end of the webinar, provide easy access to your calendar.

If you know what your step is before the sale and choose an effective strategy, it becomes easy to reverse-engineer a successful system and know exactly what needs to be done tactically by your team members. You can also find examples from noncompeting businesses that use a similar strategy and use them as a benchmark of success.

Another reason why my YouTube channel has become a successful business and a lucrative marketing strategy is because I built a marketing funnel behind my videos. What I mean by this is that when people subscribe to my channel and watch my videos, I am also showing them opportunities to take advantage of my offerings *before* the sale. I use a pre-recorded webinar (as detailed above), and, in exchange for an email address, I give away my marketing action guide for free, *and* I give them my digital magazine as an instant download on my website. You can get a copy of this at www.jendevore .rocks. That's a lot of freebies!

## Measure Only What Matters

In order to avoid "burn out" or overwhelm, it's important to create a work culture that values the individual as a whole even if you are the only person in your company. When starting a new venture, it's easy to fall into the trap of overworking. Hustle culture is especially dangerous to an individual's health.

If time is a limiting factor in your business and life, you need to know the five essential marketing campaigns every business needs. By focusing on these five core campaigns, you can do less, and get better results, than your competitors who don't know this secret to marketing success.

## Five Essential Marketing Campaigns Every Business Needs

Making the most of your marketing budget, and maximizing results, starts with knowing exactly which marketing campaigns you need and staying consistent over time. But, as a busy professional who doesn't have a lot of time to figure out what to do, it can feel overwhelming as you start a new year of planning.

To make marketing simpler, here are the Five Essential Marketing Campaigns your business needs:

1. New lead acquisition campaign
2. Referral campaign
3. Newsletter campaign
4. Follow-up and reactivation campaign
5. Internal pieces to increase customer spending campaign

Let's break them down one by one.

  **1. New Lead Acquisition Campaign**. This is the strategy for attracting and acquiring new leads at the top of your sales funnel. This target includes your online audience and community-building aspects, plus email list building to turn top-of-the-sales cycle "suspects," who are just starting the journey with you, into hand-raising, interested prospects.

2. **Referral Campaign**. These are your strategic partners who deserve a focused and thorough strategy for how you plan to stay top-of-mind with them. Don't rest on your laurels on this campaign. Plan for exactly how, when, and why you are going to ask for referrals. Create a system out of this process.

3. **Newsletter Campaign**. Do you want to get attention and stay top-of-mind with your best clients? A monthly newsletter delivered straight to their mailboxes will do the trick. Don't be boring; mix it up! Perhaps a magazine-style printed or digital newsletter fits your brand?

4. **Follow-Up and Reactivation Campaign**. Let's face it; there are many older prospects who never pulled the trigger and former clients who could still use your services. It's never too late to follow up! Create a follow-up and reactivation campaign to maximize your "return on investment" on the money you spent to attract those leads in the first place.

5. **Internal Pieces to Increase Customer Spending Campaign**. Do you have events planned for this year? What about special program offers, new product launches, or new services being added? Don't forget

to create specific campaigns to market to your internal and existing audiences.

## Measure What Matters

Generating leads is the hot button for most business owners and the area of marketing most people want to focus on first. While referrals can be an excellent way to get clients, there is a secret weapon in marketing copywriting called the Conversion Equation.

The major mistake most graphic designers and marketers make when they're building websites or designing ads is that they try to cram too much information into one experience.

Instead of sending people on a scavenger hunt, looking for the information they need from you, it's better to control the conversation on each page that you need to convert.

Here's the Conversion Equation for marketing copywriting:

- Interrupt—get their attention with a catchy headline
- Engage—let them know a solution is forthcoming on the page in your subheadline
- Educate—make your case with testimonials for emotional buyers and statistics for logical buyers
- Offer—create a compelling lead magnet as an opt-in offer and "step before the sale"

When you understand the Conversion Equation and can deploy it effectively in your marketing, you will gain a marketing superpower that will set your business on a fast track to marketing success with lead generation. But, it really is the tip of the iceberg. There are four other key outcomes to focus on and measure besides the number of leads you generate.

### Five Key Outcomes to Measure in Your Marketing

1. Number of leads generated per campaign
2. Conversion rate of leads to next step
3. Average dollar amount per transaction
4. Number of transactions per client
5. Profit margin

### How These Relate to Each Other

| | |
|---|---|
| **# LEADS GENERATED** | 1,000 |
| **CONVERSION RATE** | 10% |
| **# OF CUSTOMERS** | 100 |
| **ANNUAL TRANSACTIONS PER CUSTOMER** | 8 |
| **AVG DOLLAR AMOUNT PER TRANSACTION** | $500 |
| **ANNUAL REVENUE** | $400,000 |
| **PROFIT %** | 7% |
| **PROFIT** | $28,000 |

Kevin O'Leary from *Shark Tank* says that "knowing your numbers, profitability potential, and your ability to sell

# DO THIS NOW!

Pick an idea for a new Lead Magnet from the list below.

| ACTION GUIDE | DIGITAL MAGAZINE | EVENT |
|---|---|---|
| CHECKLIST | EBOOK | BUYER'S GUIDE |
| PRE-RECORDED WEBINAR | ASSESSMENT | DAILY CALENDAR |
| QUIZ | LIVE WEBINAR | VIDEO SERIES |

Then practice your Conversion Equation copywriting skills using the fill-in-the-blanks template below. This can be used to simplify your website homepage, build a landing page for opt-ins, create a flyer or ad, or write a social media post.

HOT BUTTON HEADLINE _____

SUPPORTING SUBHEADLINE _____

DATA POINTS: _____

_____

TESTIMONIALS: _____

_____

NAME OF ETHICAL BRIBE/LEAD MAGNET: _____

CALL TO ACTION: _____

DEADLINE: _____

your concept and self are the key factors to entrepreneurial success."

Notice how the number of social media followers, likes, or comments are not numbers that show up on the chart. Those items are vanity metrics! Sure, paying attention to your social media numbers is important to marketing success, but there are a lot of famous influencers on the internet who don't have profitable businesses because they are not measuring what *actually* matters.

In 2022, I was interviewed on VidIQs YouTube channel with over 1.36 million subscribers (at the time of this writing) because of my proven results of making big money on small channels. VidIQ is a tool that helps YouTube creators optimize their videos for search, and increase views. In my interview, I shared screenshots of my Stripe account from when I had my first $11,000 week from a channel that had less than 1,000 subscribers. At the time of this writing, my channel has just over 2,000 subscribers and business has not slowed down!

# Subscribe on YouTube
## for free, weekly
## marketing videos

WWW.YOUTUBE.COM/C/JENDEVORERICHTER

CHAPTER 7

# Now What?
# How to Implement

Ok, ok… I admit this was not the brightest idea I ever had, but one summer when I was in college, I worked at a bungee jumping tourist attraction in Destin, Florida.

It was called Air Bongo.

The idea is that you strap into a harness attached to a big, elastic cord that's tethered to a sixty-five-foot-tall tower made of steel scaffolding, and jump off—for fun.

Now, you may be thinking, "What in the world would you do that for?"

I'll tell you. It was where all the cool kids worked. So, I wanted to do it too.

My parents literally said, "If all your friends jumped off of a bridge, would you do it too?"

"Yes," I responded.

Stupid. I know.

But here's what I learned that summer at Air Bongo:

- Even scary things can be fun.

- Sometimes, we need to break the rules to truly live.
- Sometimes, taking a big leap is worth it.

That summer, I built up my bravery muscle. There wasn't anything I was afraid of back then.

I think that's served me well as a business owner and marketing consultant.

As long as you take safety precautions and check your gear, you'll be fine when you take that step off the ledge…

## Outsourcing Your Marketing Can Be Scary at First

Kids grow up watching the big brands on TV spending millions on "branding" with commercials that consist of little more than pretty videos, logos, and slogans.

But, as small business owners, we can't afford the big brand budgets. Every dollar we spend needs to be trackable, measurable, and get a result.

We can't afford to rely on "branding" alone to make the phone ring.

Usually, our competition is just mimicking what they've seen the big brands do, and following in their footsteps results in wasted money. So, if we do what everyone has always done, we're pretty much guaranteed to fail.

Making the jump from DIY to "Outsourcing Your Marketing" is the single most important jump you will ever make as a business owner.

You can do it—be brave!

# About the Author
# Jen DeVore Richter

As an invitation to join the Instant Media Mogul movement, I'd like to share a little bit more about my background so you can get to know me better and see my personal and business transformation using the same concepts you've learned in this book.

I quit my 9 to 5 job at NASA as the manager of advertising and started on this entrepreneurial journey to find more freedom and fulfillment in my life. Over the last two decades, building businesses has become my obsession.

As an entrepreneur, I started out marketing to affluent people as a high-end photographer to wealthy brides.

My other business was as an agency owner working with local mom-and-pop shops.

Now, I'm an in-demand national keynote speaker, author, and business coach serving clients all over the world, and I own a magazine publishing company of which I am the YouTube spokesperson.

Inside the Instant Media Mogul community is where I share what I've learned.

www.facebook.com/groups/instantmediamogul

My goal is to always give away better stuff for free than what other people charge for.

Yes, you heard me right, I'm giving you an amazing offer for free.

I want our relationship to start out great!

## Instant Media Mogul™

A few years ago, I got fed up with being an overworked business owner and the "best-kept secret" no one knew about. With a background that includes working as a marketing executive for NASA at Kennedy Space Center, ABC TV, and a seven-figure-earning startup company, I knew there was more for me.

Determined not to fall into the trap of starving artist with a microphone, I set out on a mission to build an expert business that not only produces a six-figure, take-home income, but also truly impacts the lives of those I serve.

Now, I am sharing my proven process for maximizing profitability in any business. I call it the Instant Media Mogul™ Process.

# FREE Offer From
# Jen DeVore Richter

Attract Your Ideal, Perfect People With Ease
With My Proven Formula

## FREE GIFT
*Companion Video Training Series*
*Downloadable Resources Included*

Claim your $233.61 worth of pure, money magnet, business-building strategies that work, ABSOLUTELY FREE.

ALL YOU HAVE TO DO IS GO HERE NOW:
www.jendevore.rocks/outsource-your-marketing-book-resources/

# URGENT PLEA!

Thank you very much for purchasing and reading my book! It really means a lot to me and my family to have your support.

I love hearing your feedback and how the ideas I've shared with you change your business and life. Hopefully, there is at least one gold nugget that you can immediately implement.

Please take a minute or two right now to leave a helpful review on Amazon, and let me (and the rest of the world) know what you found the most helpful.

OUTSOURCE
YOUR
MARKETING

SCAN ME

Thank you so much!!
**Jen DeVore Richter**

www.ingramcontent.com/pod-product-compliance
Lightning Source LLC
Chambersburg PA
CBHW060625210326

41520CB00010B/1472